DO
WORK

DO WORK

> Finding clarity, camaraderie, and progress in work and life

Max Yoder

Do Better Work is available in bulk purchases for corporate or educational use. For more information, contact dobetterwork@lessonly.com.

LLAMA Press
407 Fulton St.
Indianapolis, IN 46202
Lessonly.com

First edition, second printing: April 2019

ISBN: 978-1-7328439-0-5
eISBN: 978-1-7328439-1-2
LCCN: 2018968449

Printed in the United States of America.

Editing and production by Ben Battaglia.
Book design, illustrations, and author photo by Helen Gardner.

To Jess, who gives me clarity

To Conner, who gives me camaraderie

And to my teammates,
who forever tip the scale in Lessonly's favor

Contents

Foreword

*By Scott Dorsey, co-founder and former CEO at ExactTarget
(later Salesforce Marketing Cloud), board member at Lessonly,
and managing partner at High Alpha*

I met Max Yoder when he was 23 years old and working on
his first company, Quipol (you'll read more about that later).
It was Max's second company, Lessonly, that gave us the
opportunity to work closely together. As a board member, I've
watched Max build an extremely talented team and craft a
culture of camaraderie, clarity, and impressive growth. Max
is one of the most thoughtful and empathetic people I know,
which has led to him becoming not only an amazing leader,
but a cherished friend.

The experience I brought to Lessonly came from co-founding
and leading my own software company called ExactTarget.
We were incredibly fortunate at ExactTarget to catch the
two convergent waves of SaaS (software as a service) and the
rise of digital marketing. Our path led us to an initial public

offering on the New York Stock Exchange. Just a year later, we were acquired by Salesforce for $2.5 billion. At the time of the acquisition, we were a global company with over 2,000 employees connected by a unique culture called Orange.

Early at ExactTarget, we realized our competitive advantage was not our technology—it was our people. And our people became their very best when we created environments that completely focused on their success. This began with core values and a clear vision and mission. And it came to life through a company culture of teamwork, kindness, and a drive to win together. Our guide through it all was Jim Collins's exceptional book *Good to Great*. His description of Level 5 leadership— "humility plus will"—painted a picture of leadership I felt drawn to emulate. One of the things that drew me to Max is how he embodies Level 5 leadership. He brings a nurturing leadership style and prefers to speak about the company and contributions of others versus his own achievements.

Max's driving motivation is to care for people. Whether it's through Lessonly or its philanthropic arm, Brighter Indy, he gets energy from helping others learn, gain confidence, reduce anxiety, and become the best versions of themselves. For this reason, many people—myself included—encouraged Max to write this book and share his perspective on building better teams, doing better work, and living a better life.

As you read these pages, please note Max's emphasis on being vulnerable, sharing before you're ready, and bringing brightness to the room. His views are beautifully shared through stories, examples, and practical advice. I am enriched and inspired by Max's words, and I hope you are too. Our world needs a style of leadership that puts people at the center, and I can think of no better guide than the lessons contained in this book.

We help people do better work,
so they can live better lives.

— Lessonly Mission Statement

Introduction

Imagine a scale that measures the merit of our work. When we point a finger or ignore an issue, the scale tips left, indicating a setback. When we keep an agreement or bring energy to a project, the scale tips right, indicating progress.

Now imagine we study our moments of progress. What lessons do we learn? What behaviors come into focus? What approaches and interactions do we highlight? This book offers answers to those questions, sharing eight ways anyone can tip the scale toward progress and do better work.

The recurring themes of better work are camaraderie and clarity:

Camaraderie is a mutual trust and respect. A team has camaraderie when people are considerate, supportive, and encouraging of one another—when they want for their teammates what they want for themselves.

Clarity is a mutual understanding of what matters, why it matters, and what role each person plays in its pursuit. A team has clarity when people know what they need to do and why it's important.

When a team prioritizes camaraderie and clarity, progress is inevitable.

As you read, keep the following in mind:

If you want to see it, be it

People don't change when they are told to. They change when they are inspired and motivated to. If you want your teammates to adopt any of these lessons, your best bet is to adopt them yourself. People will notice the benefits and be inspired and motivated to follow your lead. One day, you may look up and see better work all around you. Or maybe you won't. Either way, your teammates' willingness to do better work is not in your control. What *is* in your control are your behaviors (what you do) and the behaviors you reward with your attention and support (what you celebrate). Focus there.

1% at a time, with self-compassion

These lessons are hard to learn. If you ever contradict or fall short of them, be kind to yourself and stay committed. Do what humans do best—gradually improve as you go. Identify the ideas that excite you most and get 1% better at them each day. Those little gains will become big gains if you're willing to make the investment.

It's important to be accountable for your actions. It's also important to forgive yourself along the way. Stick with it, 1% at a time, with self-compassion.

Chapter 1

Be Vulnerable

<hr>

"If you're committed to progress, you can't very well claim to have it all figured out."

—*Steven Pinker*[1]

I adore that Steven Pinker quote. It is a reminder that vulnerable people—those who acknowledge they don't have it all figured out—can be great agents of progress. They remind us that we can be confident *and* uncertain, that we can be courageous *and* need help, that "I don't know. What do you think?" is not just a seven-word reply—it's an invitation to human connection, growth, and forward motion.

These are reminders and invitations I want more people to get. This chapter is my love letter to vulnerability.

<hr>

[1] Pinker 2018, p. 14

Poe's heroic dilemma

Late one Friday night, I discussed entrepreneurship with a small group of students. Some were just starting college, others were about to graduate. All were refugees who had fled the rule of a dictator in hopes of a better life in the United States. They'd invited me to their gathering to hear what I'd learned in my attempts to start businesses.

Asking for help in moments of need was a topic that got a lot of airtime. I told the group about times when I'd done it well, times when I hadn't, and what I'd learned from the experiences. I shared how vulnerability increases communication in my life, so I can see more perspectives and come to better decisions; how it gives me room to show my teammates what I need, so they can support me more precisely; and how it encourages my teammates to do the same, so I can return the favor. I explained that good leadership is not predicated on intuitively *knowing* what to do. It's predicated on taking responsibility for *learning* what to do (chapter 2). Being vulnerable enough to ask for help accelerates that learning.

The session was open-ended, so we spent a lot of time going back and forth with questions. All but one person participated in the discussion. Poe, who I'd only met that night, didn't say a word and spent most of the session with his arms crossed. This drew me toward him. I asked Poe what was on his mind.

"About asking for help," he said, "I disagree with you. I get what you are saying, but I want to do this like a man."

I asked Poe what he meant by that, and he said a man should be able to handle pain and challenges by himself.

"He doesn't need help," Poe said, "if he's a real man."

"Where did you learn that?" I asked.

"Heroes," he said.

"What heroes?"

"Heroes in stories."

———

As the night came to a close, I learned a lot from Poe. Most of the celebrated protagonists he'd watched or read about were lone rangers with tremendous talent and destiny. Poe looked up to these characters like role models. He wanted to be as bold and brave as they were. Since he wasn't impenetrable to bullets or resistant to gravity (Poe particularly liked superheroes), he tried to model the more attainable parts of their repertoire—stoicism and self-sufficiency. Poe's heroes showed him that indecision, shame, and trauma were for the rescued, not the rescuers. Poe wanted to be a rescuer and go it alone.

You might recognize Poe's desires. I know I do. They are rooted in the Western mythos, which implies that great people dominate life, have the answer, and know the way. If you've ever modeled your behavior in pursuit of these qualities, you, Poe, and I have something in common. We feel pressure to live up to idealistic notions of heroism and human achievement—even though they are unattainable. Carrying these burdens, it's clear why so many of us struggle to acknowledge our confusion, concern, and failure. Doing so would imply we are not cut out for greatness, so we default to hiding our weaknesses. We become ashamed of our humanity. We bury the very thing that makes us accessible and motivating to others.

If we want to make progress and remain sane, we need to embrace a different model. The lone genius who blazes through difficulty unphased can no longer be our standard for excellence. Teamwork, communication, shared intelligence—these are the *profoundly human* activities that propel us forward. We owe it to ourselves, our teammates, and our children to send a clear message that it's okay to be nervous, to not know the answer, to need guidance and advice. Our camaraderie and clarity are built on these behaviors.

If we perpetuate tales of dominating life, having the answer, and knowing the way, we are not leading—we are misleading. But when we demonstrate that we struggle too, that sometimes we need help uncovering what to do or say, we can positively change people's perceptions of themselves. To struggle is to live. To learn is to live. To need one another is to live. Let's do more living.

Our psyches will thank us for the opportunity. Because when we hide our struggles for fear of losing face, it isn't just better work that suffers. Here's neuroanatomist Dr. Jill Bolte Taylor on the repercussions of repressing emotions:

> I view it like a pipe, where emotions either flow through or build up. When we choose to ignore an emotion, the need for the emotion doesn't just go away. It stays in the pipe. As we keep doing this, eventually the pipe can't handle it anymore, so it bursts. And that's when we either have an inappropriate outburst or we use an addictive behavior—like drugs or alcohol—in an attempt to cope.[2]

The good news is, as a society, we appear to be turning a corner when it comes to vulnerability. We are slowly but surely moving away from the 1950s ethos—when "Never apologize, mister! It's a sign of weakness," was considered

---

[2] Dr. Jill shared this during her keynote at Lessonly's 2018 Yellowship conference.

good advice.[3] In its place, we are applauding a more realistic, compassionate, and encouraging view of the human condition. And for good reason. We can relate to it. When we see people who make progress *and* have gaps in their armor, we are encouraged, because they remind us of ourselves.

This has—and will have—a tremendous impact at work. In the absence of vulnerability, people put pressure on themselves to appear unflappable and infallible. This results in a bunch of less-than-ideal behaviors. People say yes to things they can't reliably accomplish, act like they understand what's happening when they don't, and keep good ideas to themselves, unsure of their merit. In their worst moments, they blame others for their errors. But when we make it safe to be vulnerable, all of these negative behaviors dissipate. People realize it's okay to ask for help. They see it's safe to admit their concerns and oversights. What results is a flow of communication and understanding that helps people get on the same page, support one another, and make progress together.

---

[3] John Wayne's character, Captain Nathan Brittles, said this in the 1949 film *She Wore a Yellow Ribbon.*

Vulnerability is contagious

In early 2018, I was at a small summit with 20 other software-company CEOs. During our first session, we were asked to share the highlights and challenges we faced at work. The first 14 people, myself included, went through the motions. We spoke of uncertain investments, big revenue goals, and team dynamics. The fifteenth person, who we will call Sam, went a different direction. Sam mentioned some personal struggles that caught up to him the prior year. He told us how they'd negatively impacted his ability to manage his life and work, admitting things got pretty bad before he decided to do anything about it. Sam credited his revival to cognitive therapy. He recommended looking into similar services if any of us felt compelled.

After Sam led the way, the last five people in the group—literally every last one of them—mentioned their own personal struggles. When they were done, people who'd already spoken asked if they could share again—this time more openly. Vulnerability works like that. It's contagious. One genuine admission of struggle or confusion makes it safe for others to admit the same.

Behind so many veils of having it all together, we are starving for sincerity, some relief from our inclinations to posture. Sam demonstrated how to create a safer environment.

In a room full of people who are supposed to be (forgive me for this) "crushing it," Sam admitted fear, weakness, and a need for help. And we all followed suit. Leaders make vulnerability possible by genuinely demonstrating it.

You don't need a therapist to be vulnerable

If a grand gesture like Sam's doesn't suit you, no worries. Vulnerability can look like someone bravely revealing their darkest fears, but it can also look like someone saying, "I'm not sure," when everybody else might expect them to be. In other words, vulnerability doesn't have to be magnificent to be meaningful. Here are a bunch of everyday ways to bring more vulnerability to your team:

- Vulnerability is sharing before you're ready (chapter 2).
- Vulnerability is asking clarifying questions (chapter 4) like, "Can you elaborate a bit?" or "Do you mind sharing an example?"
- Vulnerability is telling someone what you appreciate and value about them (chapter 5).
- Vulnerability is having a difficult conversation (chapter 6) or getting an agreement (chapter 7).

- Vulnerability is asking a teammate to help you practice something.
- Vulnerability is admitting when you don't think you can get something done on time, or when you don't think you are right for a project, role, or endeavor.
- Vulnerability is owning up to a mistake. It's saying, "That is my fault, and I am sorry."
- Vulnerability is not coming into work when you're sick and need rest.

The heroes want a redo

Months after meeting Poe, I saw a DC Comics press release announcing a new miniseries called *Heroes in Crisis*. I figured it was the same old stuff—heroes fighting villains, the fate of the world hanging in the balance. But as I read more, I realized this crisis was different. It focused on the mental health ramifications of being a superhero, complete with a crisis center called Sanctuary, where "the world's greatest superheroes" go to work through their "pressures and internal conflicts."[4]

I never thought I'd cheer about superheroes needing counseling, but life is funny like that.

---

[4] DC Comics 2018

Wrapping up

Let's read that Steven Pinker quote again: "If you're committed to progress, you can't very well claim to have it all figured out."

People need to know how progress is really made. They need to see it is often messy and intimidating. They need more examples of achievement born out of support and teamwork, not isolated heroics or uncanny brilliance. They need role models who remind them that progress is possible not in spite of vulnerability, but because of it.

You and I can work to set a new tone, one human interaction at a time. We can help those who are scared know the truth: Everybody else is scared too. But with one another's help, we grow and thrive and flourish.

Chapter 2

Share Before You're Ready

Make what's getting done match what's needed.

You know what feels really good? When I work on something that ends up getting used and appreciated by others. You know what feels lousy? When I work on something that ends up unused and unappreciated by others.

I bet you can relate. We all want to do work that matters, but not all of our work resonates. There are times when we spend hours on a project, only to find we created a dud. Then there are times when the results of our efforts get snatched up like gold. I've learned the difference between duds and gold can be visualized with a simple Venn diagram. One circle is *what's getting done* and the other circle is *what's needed*.

Duds happen when what's getting done doesn't match what's needed:

In these cases, the effort we put in might be significant, but the value the rest of the team gets is minimal, because it's not what they need.

Gold happens when what's getting done matches what's needed:

So anytime we want to create something valuable, we just have to get the circles to overlap.

Communicating more is the surest way to do that. When we shorten feedback loops, allowing others to preview and inform what we're working on, we increase our odds of ending up with gold. So why don't we do that more often? Why do we risk creating duds when we don't have to?

An age-old, four-word myth is to blame. It goes like this: *Leaders know the answer.* This myth tells us great people don't need their work checked or reviewed by others, for they have enough vision and sense to hit the target unaided. It convinces us we're better off being self-reliant than asking for help.

In reality, the myth that leaders know the answer is just that—a myth. When we keep our work to ourselves, believing we should know what to do to make this project or that initiative a success, we set ourselves up for duds. The truth is, each of us has a limited vantage point. We can't see all the angles. We need one another to get closer to what's needed.

Let's rewrite the age-old myth so we can create more gold: *Leaders learn the answer.* The difference is just one word, but that one word sparks wildly different behaviors. Leaders who believe they should *know* the answer will keep things to themselves when they encounter important questions or challenges. They will look inward at the exact moment they should seek guidance. Leaders who believe they should *learn* the answer will default to asking for help and feedback. Their interactions with others will help them see more perspectives and possibilities so they can make more informed decisions.

For most of my life, I believed the myth that leaders know the answer. It was only when my first business failed that I saw the error of my ways. That first business was called Quipol.

"But why doesn't it do X?"

When I designed and developed Quipol's software, I did so in a vacuum. I made little time to get input from the people who were ultimately supposed to use it. Instead, I spent nine months bouncing ideas off of myself and those who were helping me build the software. We labored over the smallest of workflows and the most incidental details, as though we knew *exactly* how Quipol should work.

Not once did I think, *Hmm, are we piling guesses and assumptions on top of each other here?* My dreams of pulling back the curtain on Quipol and watching the world applaud my efforts were too intoxicating. My 22-year-old self couldn't see past his nose. So when Quipol's launch day finally arrived, my day of reckoning came with it.

Instead of uniform applause, the people who looked closely at Quipol instantly poked holes in my work. Literally minutes after sending a "Quipol is here" email, a question hit my inbox. It read, "Congrats on Quipol, but why doesn't it do X?" "X" was an idea that made a lot of sense, and it was something I'd never considered. Here was some guy, three minutes into his analysis of my work, noticing something I'd overlooked for *nine months*. All I could say was, "Thank you. That's a great idea. I never thought of it."

Interactions like this happened again and again. People offered great ideas, and I greatly appreciated their help. The problem was, I couldn't address any of their feedback. Those nine months in a vacuum had consumed my budget for software development. The plan was to make things perfect, remember? I didn't expect to have so many features to add, update, and remove after launch.

Quipol never recovered from my sloppy start. It lasted a year and ten months before I shut it down. Admitting failure was a soul-crushing feeling. I remember crying in my twin bed for hours, thinking, *What will I possibly do now?*

I knew one thing for sure. I was done with this whole *leaders know the answer* nonsense. I'd tried that path and found it very dissatisfying. So with Lessonly, right out of the gate we had a new mantra: We share before we're ready. Sharing before we're ready is how we put *leaders learn the answer* into practice. It's all about seeking additional perspectives as we plan and work on things.

Let's say you need to create a presentation, so you start working on the slides. If you're sharing before you're ready, you'll create simple, text-based slides that lay out the general flow of the presentation, add notes to cover what you expect to say on each slide, and then walk someone through the draft to get their feedback.

Compare this to a *leaders know the answer* approach, where you dial in every slide of your presentation before you get any feedback. Trust me, this is not a good idea. I know because I've done it. I once worked my tail off on an early draft of a presentation and wound up spending three hours on *a single slide.* I massaged phrases, finessed graphics, and dialed in typography. I was proud of myself. The next day, I took my teammate through a dry run of the deck, and he immediately pointed to my prized slide. "That looks nice," he said, "but I don't think it adds to the presentation." He explained why, and I agreed with him. We both decided to remove it. Three hours, up in smoke.

The allure of staying in a vacuum is strong, but when we make an effort to share early and often, we increase our odds of spending time on the things that are really needed, instead of the things we *think* are needed.

How to share before you're ready

Step 1. Take 30–60 minutes to create an outline or rough draft of whatever you're working on.

Step 2. Get one or more trusted reviewers to give feedback on your direction and approach. Find people who will benefit from your project's success, respect you enough to challenge your ideas, and have time to help. If you ask multiple people for feedback, seek out a blend of both veterans and newbies, as well as people who report to you and people you report to (their differing perspectives will be valuable).

Step 3. Use the feedback from your trusted reviewers to improve the direction and details of your project.

Repeat this process as needed until your work feels strong and reality-tested. This could take one review or many. It depends, so you will have to use your own judgment. If you're unsure how many feedback sessions to hold, err on the side of more.

As you practice sharing before you're ready, you'll notice the process is simple. The hard part is having the courage to do it.

"Often it's enough that they are not you."

In his writing handbook, *The Sense of Style,* Steven Pinker encourages his own version of sharing before you're ready. Pinker recognizes the process of sharing early drafts "sounds banal but is in fact profound." He writes:

> Social psychologists have found that we are overconfident, sometimes to the point of delusion, about our ability to infer what people think, even the people who are closest to us. Only when we ask those people do we discover what's obvious to us isn't obvious to them. That's why professional writers have editors. It's also why politicians consult polls, why corporations hold focus groups, and why Internet companies use A/B testing. . . . [A]sk a roommate or colleague or family member to [review your work] and comment on it. Your reviewers needn't even be a representative sample of your intended audience. Often it's enough that they are not you.[1]

---

[1] Pinker 2014, p. 75

Frequently asked questions about sharing before you're ready

What if I disagree with the feedback I get?

You are not obligated to take action on feedback that does not seem thoughtful or productive. If somebody gives you feedback and you're not sure if you agree with it, seek out additional opinions—or ask, "What do you base that feedback on?" If their response is, "My gut!" you be the judge of whether their gut is a good one to follow.

Also remember a voice is not a vote. This is especially important for managers. You should hear people out, but if you're a manager, your work isn't an exercise in democracy. Sometimes, you will have to make hard calls that won't be supported by a popular vote. People might want to stick with the old way because it's easier than the new way, even when the new way is in their best interest. In these moments, remember you get to make the final decision, so make it. Just be sure to get feedback from your team before you do. And if you end up going against the grain, explain why. People deserve to know the reasons behind your decisions.

How early in a project is too early to get feedback?

If you don't know where to start, you're ready for feedback. Tell others so they can help. But if you think you know where to start, get a quick draft going and then seek feedback.

A sculpting analogy also helps me with this question. Early in a project, a seasoned sculptor will create and share models that demonstrate what they are thinking. When the sculptor's trusted reviewer says, "I love it, but I think the chin could use more dimension," the sculptor can easily reshape the chin, since everything is still wet and pliable. The sculptor doesn't wait until their final product has been cast in bronze to see what others think. At that point, it's too late. Mustering the energy to go back and rework the chin—forget about it. Be like a sculptor. Seek feedback in the clay stages. Don't wait until your project is figuratively bronzed to get keen eyes on it.

Wrapping up

Individually, each of us has a limited perspective, but together we are a force to be reckoned with. Sharing before we're ready is how we get outside the vacuum of our minds so we can see more of what's possible. It's how we demonstrate and spread a healthier model of leadership, one where people are comfortable asking questions and learning the answer. It's how we make *what's getting done* match *what's needed*.

It's how we bring more gold to the people who count on us.

Chapter 3

Look for Opportunity

Challenges are inevitable, but the way
we respond to them is a choice.

At work, unexpected things will happen. You'll be cruising
along just fine when—all of a sudden—your plan hits a dead
end. You'll have to go back to the drawing board and reassess your efforts. Some teammates will have to start over completely. And that deadline you all expected to hit . . . it's not
looking good.

So what do you do?

In moments like these, when things don't go how we want
them to, we get to tell ourselves one of two stories:

The first story focuses on the potential downside. This is
called the **threat story**. It happens when we encounter a challenge and tell ourselves, *This is really bad*. Threat stories assume
unexpected deviations from the plan are generally negative and

should be minimized. If we tell ourselves a lot of threat stories, we develop a **threat mindset**.

The second story is the **opportunity story**, which focuses on the potential upside of a challenge. Opportunity stories do not assume unexpected deviations from the plan are necessarily bad. Instead, they recognize detours are bound to occur and can be beneficial. When we tell ourselves opportunity stories, they sound like this: *Well, that's not what I hoped would happen, but that's okay. The initial plan wasn't necessarily the best plan. It was just the initial plan, and now I need a new one. If I try hard enough, I bet I can turn this so-called problem into a good thing.* When we tell ourselves a lot of opportunity stories, we develop an **opportunity mindset**.

Thought it was bad, but it was good

Take a minute to do a self-reflection exercise. Try to remember a time when you assumed a rejection, delay, or change was negative, only to realize it just made things *different*—not necessarily *worse*. Ideally, you'll recall a time when the difference wound up benefiting you.

When I do this exercise, three particular moments come to mind. There was the time I received back-to-back rejections for two stellar job opportunities, the time my girlfriend left me, and the time Quipol failed. Each of these moments reminds me of a hard but important truth: Not getting what I want can pan out well.

The two job rejections meant I was available when a third possibility came along. That one turned into a job offer from a stranger named Kristian Andersen. Kristian went on to become my greatest mentor and perennial business partner.

The girlfriend leaving me brought another woman into my life. Her name is Jess. I am now her husband and she is my greatest gift. Kristian married us in front of our family and friends in 2017.

My failure with Quipol gave me a chance to try again with Lessonly. The first person I asked to join me was a guy named Conner Burt. During Quipol, I knew Conner by reputation only. But through our partnership at Lessonly, he's become my dearest friend. Conner served as the best man in my wedding, handing the rings to Kristian before Jess and I said, "I do."

Given the choice, I would have wanted the initial job opportunities to turn into offers, the girlfriend to stay, and Quipol to succeed. Now, with distance from the heat of these moments and the benefit of hindsight, I am so grateful they turned out the way they did.

My point is this: Behind every apparent bad break, there is a potential breakthrough. We just have to be willing to look for it.[1] In my experience, few stories capture this reality better than the making of *Jaws*.

"The shark is not working."

As soon as Steven Spielberg took the helm of *Jaws*, he went against the wishes of everyone around him and decided to film the movie on location at Martha's Vineyard. Executives at Universal Studios implored him not to take the risk, but he was young and determined, so he did it anyway.

"That decision haunted us that entire summer," said *Jaws* production executive Bill Gilmore. "We fought the Atlantic Ocean day after day after day. And many is the day that we came back with our tail between our legs."[2]

All the while, Spielberg was making edits to the one thing he *could* control—the script. He and his team reworked the story every night, trying to come up with the next day's material. For some of the cast and crew, these last-minute

---

[1] In sharing my stories—writing about life events, working to find positive meaning in them—I am practicing reappraisal. Reappraisal can be massively beneficial to a person's mental health (Pals & McAdams, 2004). If past adversity is lingering in your mind and you want to turn it into a growth catapult, read *Opening Up by Writing It Down* by James Pennebaker and Joshua Smyth.

[2] Goldberg 2010

changes were stimulating. For others, they sparked anxious questions: *When will the revisions stop? Do they actually know how to make this movie?*

Finally, there was the mechanical shark. It was unquestionably a mess. "Wherever you were on the island," said Richard Dreyfuss, who played Matt Hooper in the film, "you could hear the radio mics, and they were always saying, 'The shark is not working.' "[3]

This was a movie about a shark, and there wasn't one. "The superstar was going to be the shark. That was at least my plan going in,"[4] Spielberg recalled in a documentary on the film. "The script was filled with shark. Shark here, shark there, shark everywhere."[5]

Weather issues and an ever-changing script are enough to put genuine doubt in the collective mind of any production. Add to that an unworkable star of the show and you have a recipe for dread. Crew members began asking when they could go home. Producer Richard Zanuck worked behind the scenes to keep Universal executives from firing Spielberg. "Threats

---

[3] Turner 2010
[4] Goldberg 2010
[5] Lacy 2017

were going back and forth every day," Zanuck said. "They were very, very concerned that this was out of control."[6]

In an interview during the filming of *Jaws*, Spielberg admitted to feeling the heat:

> At times, especially when you're by yourself at night, it weighs more heavily than during the working day when your mind is on getting good film. And sometimes at night you realize that it's a great responsibility and you're juggling a lot of cash and it's sometimes very frightening.[7]

With the shark showing no sign of improvement, Spielberg had two choices: He could tell himself a threat story, tender his resignation, and try to salvage whatever remained of his career. Or he could look for opportunity and try to make a movie about a shark *without* a shark to show.

"I had no choice but to figure out how to tell the story without the shark," Spielberg said. "I went back to Alfred Hitchcock—[asking myself,] 'What would Alfred Hitchcock do in a situation like this?' . . . [I realized it's] what we don't see that is really truly frightening."[8]

---

[6] Goldberg 2010
[7] Ibid.

Spielberg went back to a technique they'd used in an earlier scene, where the shark, which was barely visible, became entangled in a barrel. The barrel was then dragged across the top of the water, suggesting the shark's movement below. It was an effective technique. Spielberg looked for more ways to get the shark caught up in everyday objects—be it a person, a pier, or a rope. Combining this approach with reaction shots and John Williams's iconic score—*dun dun, dun dun*—Spielberg and his crew found a way to trade a visual shark for something much scarier—the audience's imagination.

"All these moments," said Spielberg, "[were] kind of divine providence saying, 'There's another way—a better way—to make this movie. And I better listen.' And I did. I listened to the muses."[9]

When *Jaws* hit theaters in the summer of 1975, it surged with success, breaking attendance records and becoming the highest-grossing film of its time.[10] It was hailed as a masterpiece of suspense and tension, changing the lives of everyone who worked on it—as well as those who simply saw it.

[8] Goldberg 2010
[9] Ibid.
[10] Hendrek 1976

In the end, the shark was visible for just four minutes of the film's 124-minute runtime. If *Jaws* isn't an example of looking for opportunity in challenge, I don't know what is.

Practical ways to foster an opportunity mindset at work

Lessonly board member and former ExactTarget CEO Scott Dorsey has a way of keeping everyone around him opportunity-focused, no matter the height of the hurdle or the size of the setback.

Whenever one of Lessonly's big plans hits a dead end, Scott responds the exact same way. He rubs his hands together, signaling excitement, and asks, "Okay, what are our alternatives?" Then, he picks up a whiteboard marker and leads an exercise:

Step 1. We decide if the original goal is still the right goal. Once we decide on the right goal, we formulate a list of alternative plans.

Step 2. We whittle down the list to the three alternative plans that have the most potential.

Step 3. We pick the best alternative plan and that becomes the new plan for hitting our goal.

Every time Scott leads this exercise, I feel my energy rebuilding. In the moment, he doesn't fault us for our errors or let us sulk in our sorrows. Instead, he focuses on reclaiming momentum and progress.

Days or weeks later, Scott might pull me or Conner aside to suggest ways we could have avoided the dead end in the first place, but he is excellent about waiting until we've picked a new course of action to give this type of advice. Scott knows Conner and I don't need a lecture right after we make a mistake. Instead, what we need is someone who can help us move forward again. When we are back in a position of positivity and excitement, we can take Scott's more critical feedback, so that's when he gives it to us.

Moments like these make it easy to see how Scott led ExactTarget to become a multi-billion-dollar company. He knows how to interpret reality in a way that brings forward motion and possibility back to mind.

Wrapping up

Next time you run into competitive pressures, execution errors, or acts of God, remember what separates those who do better work from those who wallow in self-pity: They look at a challenging life event, a sinking shark, or a dead-end plan and find the opportunity within it.

Chapter 4

Ask Clarifying Questions

To be sure
You understand,
Ask for more.
Raise your hand.

I know people who treat their intuition like a finite resource, conserving it for moments when it's required. In all other occasions, when more clarity is possible, they ask for it. They probe for potential nuance. They ask questions about questions. In doing so, they show respect for the topic at hand and demonstrate their desire to positively contribute to it.

I want to be more like these people, and I want you to be too. We have the power to change our lives and our work by asking more clarifying questions. We don't have to be so reliant on our intuition. We don't have to guess our way to understanding. We can help ourselves and others get to "I get it." All we have to do is spend more time raising our hands. So how do we motivate ourselves to do that?

Two things keep me vigilant:

1. We are all cursed

We all live under the curse of knowledge.[1] It's a psychological phenomenon where we assume everyone has learned the same things we have. It turns out that once we know something, it becomes hard to imagine *not* knowing it, so we unwittingly treat others as if they have the same background information we do. When we omit specific details as though they were obvious, or use acronyms and jargon as though they were everyday English, that's the curse of knowledge at work. Knowing we are all prone to under-explanation keeps me motivated to ask clarifying questions.

2. Life is not a TV show

You've probably seen an Aaron Sorkin drama. He wrote *The West Wing*, *The Newsroom*, *The Social Network*, and *A Few Good Men*, among many other shows and movies. Sorkin is famous for his characters' whip-smart dialogue. In the worlds

---

[1]   Froyd & Layne 2008

he creates, people process information with cocaine quickness and calculator precision. They are ready in milliseconds with retorts that are both forthright and sharp. It's impressive stuff! It leaves you thinking Sorkin's characters—no matter how exhausting or unrealistic—are *smart*.

I think we fail to ask clarifying questions because we want to look smart too. We want to appear as savvy as characters in a well-written drama.

The problem is, life is not a TV show. When we act like we get it because we think we should, we allow for miscommunication that is entirely avoidable. Our goal as teammates is to get everybody on the same page. So next time you hear a vague question or statement, rather than being the person who wants to look impressive, be the person who keeps everyone aligned. Ask clarifying questions over and over again until the matter isn't so vague anymore.

Here are some examples of this behavior

What follows are everyday snippets of conversations that choose clarifying questions over assumption. For these examples, know two things:

1. Tom is the typical teammate. He makes statements and asks questions that leave room for interpretation.
2. Lena is the model. She demonstrates how to help Tom trade nuance for clarity.

Example I

> **Tom:** I'm not convinced it's worth it.
>
> **Lena:** That's good to know. Can you elaborate a bit on why you think that?

The assumptive response would be, "I agree," or "I disagree." The clarifying response seeks to understand Tom's viewpoint. Tom might have information Lena doesn't. She'll never know unless she asks.

Example II

> **Tom:** We need to make some changes here soon.
>
> **Lena:** What sort of changes?

The assumptive response would be, "Okay," or "Got it." The clarifying response asks Tom to expand on what he means. Without context, "we need to make some changes" is an ominous thing to hear. Lena helps Tom clear up the ambiguity.

Example III

> **Tom:** I'll follow up on that.

Lena: Thank you! Can we review your findings during our meeting on Thursday?

The assumptive response would be, "Great, thanks." The clarifying response seeks to replace unclear expectations with an agreed-upon plan. (In chapter 7, we'll discuss agreements in detail.)

Example IV

Tom: Are you going to move forward with that?

Lena: Currently, yes. But I'm still open to ideas. Do you have any thoughts or recommendations?

The assumptive response is "Yes, I am," or "No, I'm not." The clarifying response takes a breath to understand what's motivating Tom's question, so Lena can ensure she's not missing something.

Example V

Tom: How long is the meeting?

Lena: It's an hour. Is there anything on your mind I can help with?

The assumptive response would be, "It's an hour." The clarifying response seeks to understand why Tom is asking. Maybe he's nervous about a competing priority. Some people need encouragement to share more. Lena is giving Tom a chance to speak up in case anything else is on his mind.

Example VI

Tom: Mike is worried about it.

Lena: What do you base that on?

The assumptive response would be, "Thanks for letting me know," or "Got it." The clarifying response seeks to understand if Tom is *guessing* how Mike feels, or if he actually *knows* how Mike feels.

Example VII

Tom: You should check it out. It's eye-opening.

Lena: Thanks, I will! What did you find eye-opening about it?

The assumptive response would be, "Thanks, I will!" The clarifying response helps Lena understand what she should focus on when she checks out Tom's recommendation.

Example VIII

Tom: Can we get an SME on our API?

Lena: Can you explain what SME and API mean?

The assumptive response would be to nod at these opaque acronyms and then Google them later. The clarifying response asks Tom to explain his jargon, because dang, Tom, this is hard to follow.

———

Some people will read these everyday examples and think, *Look, Max, when it comes to the small stuff, I don't have time for extra questions. But when something is really important, believe me, I'll ask for clarity. Until then, I have work to do.*

Here's my two-part response:

First, the small stuff matters a lot. Many big misalignments are born out of little misalignments that get compounded over time. Save yourself the later trouble now.

Second, if you're not training to be more thoughtful during everyday interactions, what makes you think you'll be more thoughtful during crunch time? Training is all about learning how to do things *before* the heat of the moment so you'll be prepared to do them *during* the heat of the moment. Think of these everyday interactions like exercise. They build the muscles you'll need when urgency and pressure increase. In those moments, clarifying questions can be the difference between a hasty decision and a good call. Don't skip daily practice and expect to play well in the big game.

It never hurts to explain why you're asking clarifying questions, especially if you're asking a lot of them. Connect the dots for people. Say things like, "I want to make sure I understand this well. May I ask a few questions?"

Take clarifying questions with you everywhere you go

Clarifying questions aren't just beneficial to our teammates. They foster richer and clearer connections with everybody we meet.

Consider customer interactions. Next time a current or prospective customer asks a question like, "Do you have [that fancy feature that your competitor has]?" don't presume they see value in the feature simply because they brought it up. People ask about unimportant things all the time. Maybe they are checking an inconsequential box on an evaluation form, or they noticed a lull in the conversation and wanted to break the silence. Maybe they're asking because they don't really understand the merit of the feature and they want your perspective on how valuable it actually is. To find out for sure, just say, "That feature can mean different things to different people. I'm curious . . . what makes you ask about it?"

In all likelihood, the person will tell you what's behind their question, and then you'll know. You might get less-than-ideal news. They might say the feature is somehow vital to their plans. But at least you've replaced presumption with good information. Better still, by asking more questions, you will learn *why* the feature is so important. This will be helpful information as you continue the conversation.

In any relationship, in any situation, clarifying questions can help you see the world through the eyes of others, and there's always something to be gained from that.

Here are three more clarifying questions that make my heart sing

"What's our goal here?"

At Lessonly, we sometimes forget to set clear goals for our projects and initiatives. We assume everyone is on the same page about why we are working on something, so we jump right to the planning stage. It's important to plan—to account for things like to-dos, timelines, and divisions of labor. But it's more important to clarify the goal.

The goal aligns and liberates us. It shows us what matters most and reminds us our plan isn't the only path to success. It's just one potential path to it (chapter 3). So whenever I hear someone push their teammates to clarify the goal of a meeting or initiative, I know we are setting ourselves up to do better work.

If you ever ask, "What's our goal here?" and get an answer that doesn't feel like much of a goal, ask, "Can you help me understand why that matters?" Repeat this question until you get to the fundamental reason everybody was brought together. After all, if we don't know why we are working on something, should we be working on it?

"Have we talked to anyone who has tried this before?"

There are a lot of people in this world. Chances are, the thing we are considering has been tried before, and we might know someone who knows someone who already gave it a go. The goal of this question is *not* to use someone else's experience as a perfect proxy for ours. An initiative can fail with one team and succeed with another. The goal is to be more informed about the experiences of others so we can apply any relevant learnings to our efforts.

"Can someone repeat back what they just heard me say? I want to make sure I'm being clear."

Did your explanation make sense or confuse everyone? This will help you find out. When we ask others to clarify what they are hearing us say, the curse of knowledge is naturally weakened. Just be sure you include the last part about testing your ability to be clear, so your teammates know you're not testing their ability to listen. And feel free to ask others if you can repeat what you heard them say. That works well too!

Wrapping up

More clarity won't always be available. In those moments, your intuition will be precious. But in other scenarios, when more clarity is just a conversation or email away, you know what to do. Ask more questions.

At first, it might feel uncomfortable to be the person who assumes less than others. But consider how respectful it is to seek to understand someone *before* you give your thoughts. And remember how much you are helping those who look up to you when you practice this approach. You're showing them that wise people don't guess when they don't have to.

Chapter 5

Highlight What's Working

"Life offers so many chances to use one tool instead of another, and often you can use a strength to get around a weakness."

—*Jonathan Haidt* [1]

It is natural to focus on problems. So when we have a choice to pay attention to what's working or what's not, most of us over-index on the latter. It's how we're wired[2] and it's what we know.[3] We know how to find problems, we know how to identify their causes, and we know how to solve them. When

---

[1] Haidt 2006, p. 169
[2] Ito, Larsen, et al. 1998
[3] Haidt 2006, pp. 29, 37, 54

it comes to focusing on what's working, though, it's a different story. We tend to see things that are working as boxes already checked and missions already accomplished. We devote less attention to these areas because they are "taken care of."

This oversight is not a small one. When we overdo it on problem solving, we run the risk of missing the very thing we're after—the behaviors that lead to success. Where our problems tell us what *not to do,* what's working tells us what *to do.* And it's what *to do* that matters. I could give you a list of things to avoid, but you're better off with a list of things that reliably do the trick. When we focus on what's working, we learn how to identify and reverse-engineer that list so it can be shared and applied more widely.

The goal of this chapter is to encourage you to override your natural inclination to focus on what's not working, so you can spend less time playing whack-a-mole with your problems and more time highlighting and learning from the things that are going well.

My path on this journey started with a methodology developed by David Cooperrider and Suresh Srivastva. Allow me to introduce you to appreciative inquiry.

An introduction to appreciative inquiry

In 1967, management guru Peter Drucker published *The Effective Executive,* positing that teams accomplish great things not by eliminating their weaknesses, but by cultivating and aligning their strengths to such a degree that their weaknesses become irrelevant.[4] Just as a car moves forward not by banishing inertia but by overwhelming it with energy, teams move forward not by banishing their problems but by overwhelming them with their strengths.

At its core, appreciative inquiry is a framework for applying Drucker's wisdom.[5] It encourages us to spend more time focusing on our strengths by asking and answering simple questions like, "What's going well around here, and how do we do more of it?" As we pose these positive questions, we expose what's working so more people can learn from it.

What follows are my favorite aspects of appreciative inquiry.

Appreciative inquiry is grounded in reality

Appreciative inquiry helps us search our past for the good things our teammates have done. Then it encourages us to lift those things up like baby Simba.

---

4 Drucker 1967, p. 71
5 Kay 2016

For example, if our teammate Laura did something we are grateful for, we should gather the team and let them know:

Hey, everybody, we would like to give a shoutout to Laura. A few days ago, a client called and was very upset. We accidentally missed our end of an agreement and forgot to give them advance notice. Laura volunteered to handle the issue and did so impressively. She came to the conversation ready with an apology and two new courses of action for the client to choose from. She never passed the buck, acted defiantly, or rolled her eyes at the client's anger. The client emailed us later that day and specifically said how thankful they were for the way Laura approached things. Let's give it up for Laura![6]

This sort of celebration is as much for the rest of the team as it is for Laura. It offers a tangible and grounded example of what better work looks like. It's not some anecdote about Michael Jordan or another impossibly accomplished person. It's a story about Laura—the person who sits right next to you and deals with the same stuff you do. It didn't happen in

---

[6] Some shoutouts are light on details, making them hard to learn from and replicate. This shoutout shares particulars, so those who are listening can understand what made Laura's behavior exemplary.

game seven of the playoffs and it wasn't some miraculous feat. It happened a few days ago, on a regularly scheduled business day. The proximity of the progress is the power of it. Laura set an example that all of us can reach. All we have to do is *choose* to reach it.

I believe people want to do their jobs well. The main reason they don't is they lack concrete examples of what it looks like to do their jobs well. Appreciative inquiry helps us identify and share concrete examples of doing a job well so more people end up doing exactly that.

Appreciative inquiry helps us reverse-engineer our successes

A Lessonly manager walked into my office with a problem. A recurring handoff from one department to the next was breaking down and she didn't know what to do about it.

I used an appreciative inquiry technique for reframing the conversation to better understand what we were after: "Can you tell me about a time when one of these handoffs went really well?" She immediately shared an example. This made it easy for us to see what we were aiming for (handoffs that go well), as opposed to what we weren't (handoffs that break down).

Two more questions helped us reverse-engineer her positive example: "What were the circumstances that led to that handoff going well? What were you and others doing that made it possible?" The manager began to recount the interactions and behaviors that preceded the handoff. We noted them as she went: "Marshall did this, and then Dominique did that." By the time she was done, we had a recipe for making handoffs go smoothly. We left the headspace of *this thing is broken* and found the headspace of *we know how to make this work.*

After our meeting, the manager got the departments together and reviewed what a good handoff looks like. She reminded the group why specific elements of a handoff are important to everyone's success. Sure enough, as more people came to understand why handoffs matter and how to do them, future handoffs got smoother and smoother.

This manager was also thoughtful about revisiting the handoff process every couple of months. She didn't assume everyone would remember everything she'd said during the handoff review. Instead, she continued to focus on the topic because it continued to matter. That's good leadership—if it still matters, keep saying it. Once people begin playfully mocking you about the topic, you'll know you're getting through.

Appreciative inquiry helps us zoom out

I remember being frustrated with a teammate and seeking counsel from Conner. He listened intently as I explained what was on my mind. When I was done, he suggested we switch gears for a minute and compare my frustrations with a list of things the teammate was doing well. It seemed like we went on for ten minutes building that "going well" list. That's when I realized how myopically I'd been viewing things. I was focusing on a couple of things that weren't going how I wanted, instead of the majority of things that were. It was not a fair assessment of my teammate.

These days, when I am uneasy, overwhelmed, or irritated with something or someone, I make a list that answers the question, "What's going well?" When I line up what's going well with what isn't, I regain perspective on how much progress is being made, even as some aspects remain more challenging than I'd like.[7]

---

[7] If you want to begin building your appreciative muscle, here are two things you can do: 1. Take ten minutes once a week to write down three things you appreciate. Over time, you'll notice it becoming easier and easier to spot things you appreciate in your everyday life. 2. When someone says or writes something about you that makes you proud, add it to a document called "Nice Things People Said." I've been doing this for years, and I love it. When I find myself drifting toward self-judgment, I read excerpts from the document to remind myself that I have redeeming qualities too. For me, frequent self-doubt is a fact of life. Keeping a "Nice Things People Said" document is a low-effort, high-yield way to shoo that doubt away and remember my strengths.

Appreciative inquiry encourages us to offer and ask for specifics

To maximize the value of your appreciation, call out the *specific* things you appreciate and explain why they matter.

For example, imagine you're in a meeting and your teammate just gave a fantastic presentation. Instead of simply saying, "That was great work," take an additional moment to explain *why* it was such great work. You might add, "Your examples resonated with me because you tied each one back to a team objective, and that helped me understand why I should pay attention and invest in this project."

Alternatively, when someone tells you, "Thanks!" or "Great job!" or "I loved it!" don't be shy about asking them for more detail. Say, "Thanks for saying so. I really appreciate the feedback. If you're comfortable sharing, what in particular resonated with you?" People may highlight details you weren't even aware of.

In every case, the value of positive feedback is much greater when we know what's propelling it.

A note on problems

As Sue Annis Hammond reminds us in *The Thin Book of Appreciative Inquiry*, when someone is having a heart attack, they don't want to hear how healthy their other arteries are. They want someone to save their life![8]

This is a funny way of reminding us that diagnosing and solving problems will always be important. Matters of compliance are a good example of this. If somebody or something is noncompliant and putting others at risk, diagnosing the problem and solving it is a very good idea.

Don't think of appreciative inquiry as an all-or-nothing proposition. If you're currently focusing on problems 80% of the time, commit to spending more time each day highlighting what's working. Who knows, maybe you'll like how 70% feels! It sure won't hurt to find out.

Wrapping up

Our choices about what we pay attention to are life-defining. Next time you look around your team (or your family or friend group), make more time to ask yourself and others, "What's going well around here, and how do we do more of it?" If your experience is anything like mine, this shift in perspective will be positively life-changing.

---

[8] Hammond 2013, p. 7

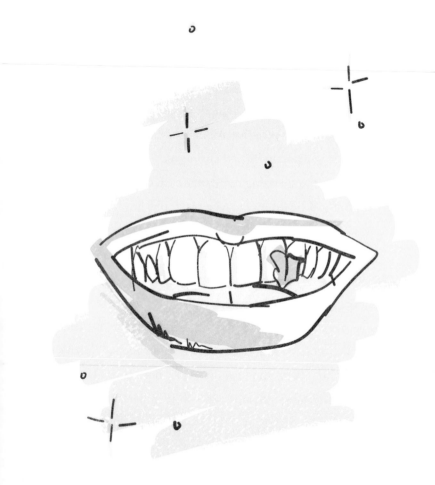

Chapter 6

Have Difficult Conversations

Turn conflict into
compassion and progress.

When a person notices something in my teeth, I want them to tell me. Otherwise, I could spend all day going about my business with no idea how embarrassing I look until I finally end up in front of a mirror.

In life, we have mirrors for our faces, but not for our behaviors. So when we do things that others consider unfortunate, off-putting, or ineffective, we depend on them to say something. Otherwise, the behavior is figuratively in our teeth, and we run a greater risk of taking it with us everywhere we go.

I appreciate the people who tell me when something is stuck in my actual teeth, and I appreciate those who speak up when they think something is in my behavioral teeth.

If I unintentionally hurt someone or overlook something important, I want to know. So when people choose a difficult conversation over a passed buck ("I thought someone else would say something"), an uncharitable posture ("He should just *know* how annoying that is"), or pseudo-compassion ("I don't want to hurt Max's feelings"), I am impressed and grateful. They are doing the hard thing and proving they care about me.

I am aware that most of us are ill-equipped for difficult conversations. When conflict arises, we fall to the level of our training, and our training isn't very impressive. Since many of us don't have the tools to deal with conflict, we default to the behaviors that were modeled to us:

- We talk to people who aren't involved in the situation so we can vent and feel more justified about our side of things. *"I know, right? Can you believe they'd do that?"*
- We act like nothing happened, repressing our feelings and hoping for the situation to resolve itself. *It's fine.*
- We villainize the other side of the situation and begin to interpret their future behaviors through a less-than-charitable lens. *What an awful person.*
- We confront the situation with hurtful language. *"You are being a jerk!"*

- We resort to intimidation or physical violence.

  They'll think twice about ever doing that again . . .

We need better tools to work through conflict. And while we're at it, we need a clearer understanding of conflict's value. If we can stop our frustrations from festering and dividing us, we can free ourselves from distress and find more camaraderie and clarity in our lives. Instead of just hoping the other person will course-correct because of our subtle, passive cues, we can talk to one another. And we should. Better relationships, better work, and a better world—they are all possible, but only if we are willing to work through the harder stuff with empathy and communication.

Rethinking conflict

When I was younger, I had the wrong idea about conflict. I thought it was inherently bad—something to avoid at all costs. I see now that conflict is a fact of life and a great catalyst for personal and relational growth. To understand where my misperception of conflict came from, I sought counseling and good books.

Here's what counseling taught me: Growing up, the conflict I witnessed led to arguments, and those arguments led to a host of unfortunate outcomes—resentments grew, friendships ended, divorces commenced. With these as my examples, it's no surprise that I equated conflict with dysfunction. I didn't realize that conflict wasn't the problem. The *arguments* were the problem.

Here's what good books taught me: Argument is war.[1] Just look at the language we use to describe our arguments:

"She defended her position."
"He shot that down."
"She attacked his weakest point."
"He dropped a bomb."
"She gave ground."
"He surrendered."

It's no wonder arguments are often explosive and damaging. When we let conflict lead us into something that is modeled after war, we aren't likely to find peace.

Fortunately, there's another way. Instead of arguing our way to fatigued and fragile relationships, we can choose to create antifragile relationships.

---

[1] Lakoff & Johnson 1980, p. 4

Antifragile relationships

If you've never heard the word *antifragile*, that's because it's pretty new. Nassim Taleb coined it in his 2012 book by the same name, explaining that things in life are either fragile, robust, or antifragile.[2] A glass vase is an example of something fragile. Drop it enough times—maybe even once—and you'll break it. Some things are robust, like a metal pipe. You can handle it aggressively and it won't get any better or worse. Other things are antifragile, meaning they improve under pressure. The human body is a great example of this. Put it through a workout or give it a taste of some germs, let it rest for a bit, and the next thing you know, it's stronger! With muscles, antibodies, and other antifragile things, acute stress leads to growth and improvement.

I bring this up because the way we approach conflict makes our relationships either fragile or antifragile. When we choose repression, avoidance, or argument, we put our relationships in states of chronic stress—making them fragile over time. When we choose compassionate communication, we learn about ourselves and one another. This learning brings

---

[2] Taleb 2012, pp. 20–23

understanding and improvement to our relationships—making them antifragile over time.

It's *scary* to face conflict and have difficult conversations, but that's exactly *why* we need to do it. The acute stress helps us grow and serve one another better. Our relationships deserve that.

Conflict will always be with us. Let's learn how to make it useful.

The art of nonviolent communication

Nonviolent communication (NVC) is a process developed by the late Dr. Marshall Rosenberg. It was designed to help us have richer and more productive difficult conversations. Using NVC, we learn to explain what we're observing, how it makes us feel, and what we need. If just one person in a difficult conversation applies the fundamentals of NVC, that conversation is apt to go better. Never forget that. All it takes is *one* empathetic person to change the tempo of a tense situation.

At Lessonly, every teammate gets a copy of Rosenberg's book, *Nonviolent Communication: A Language of Life*. When we first introduced the book to the team, there wasn't much excitement. The general vibe was, *What the heck is nonviolent communication? And please tell me it's a quick read.* Then some brave teammates started trying it out—mostly at home—and sharing their success stories. The next thing we knew, even reluctant people were cracking the book open.

These days, as new people join the team and start reading *Nonviolent Communication*, I repeatedly hear, "Oh, wow, this makes so much sense." In more than six years at Lessonly, nothing we've shared with the team has resulted in such widespread, positive feedback. Here are a few notes people sent me after reading the book:

"How many issues in my life have been entirely centered around an inability to do this? Maybe all of them. Incredibly helpful."

"I am not known as a good communicator but I practiced nonviolent communication with someone this week and it worked! They listened and heard me. This is one of the best books I've read."

"I just bought another copy for my husband. We need more of this at home."

Nonviolent communication gives us the tools we need to work through—and benefit from—the conflict in our lives. And while I would stop short of calling it easy—the process asks us to replace many old habits, and that is never easy—it is not complicated. It's something you *will* get the hang of, if you want to.

There is no way to synthesize all of Dr. Rosenberg's wisdom into a single chapter. But with his estate's permission, I've outlined some of NVC's key concepts so you can, slowly but surely, begin using them in your conversations. Ideally, as you see results, you will be motivated to pick up his book and read the whole thing. Just take time with it and don't give up. The investment is worth it.

The basics of nonviolent communication

Here's how Rosenberg breaks down the four components of the NVC process:

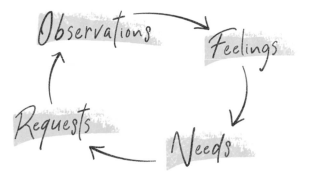

© Marshall Rosenberg from *Nonviolent Communication* 3rd edition.
For more information, visit www.nonviolentcommunication.com.

1. Observations

"First, we observe what is actually happening in a situation: what are we observing others saying or doing that is either enriching or not enriching our life? The trick is to be able to articulate this observation without introducing any judgment or evaluation—to simply say what people are doing that we either like or don't like."

2. Feelings

"Next, we state how we feel when we observe this action: are we hurt, scared, joyful, amused, irritated?"

3. Needs

"Thirdly, we say what needs of ours are connected to the feelings we have identified. . . . For example, a mother might express these three pieces to her teenage son by saying, 'Felix, when I see two balls of soiled socks under the coffee table and another three next to the TV, I feel irritated, because I am needing more order in the rooms that we share in common.' "

4. Requests

"She would follow immediately with the fourth component—a very specific request: "Would you be willing to put your socks in your room or in the washing machine?" The fourth component addresses what we are wanting from the other person that would enrich our lives."[3]

NVC asks us to express these four components as clearly as we can, while also working to identify them in the words and actions of others. Rosenberg arranged the components in a linear order, but he clarifies that we can communicate compassionately without expressing all of them every time. The goal is to focus on the four components—and help others do the same—until we establish a flow of communication and understanding between one another.

Sharing observations without judgment

I can handle you telling me
What I did or didn't do.
And I can handle your interpretations,
But please don't mix the two.

If you want to confuse any issue,
I can tell you how to do it:

---

[3] Rosenberg 2015, p. 6

Mix together what I do
With how you react to it.

—Marshall B. Rosenberg, PhD[4]

Rosenberg stresses the importance of decoupling our observations (what we see) from our evaluations (our judgments of what we see):

> The Indian philosopher J. Krishnamurti once remarked that observing without evaluating is the highest form of human intelligence. . . . When we combine observation with evaluation, we decrease the likelihood that others will hear our intended message. Instead, they are apt to hear criticism and thus resist whatever we are saying.[5]

An *observation* highlights a specific and concrete fact:

- Mary, *during the team meeting, you said I was slowing you down.*
- Paul, *you have not closed a deal in seven months.*

---

[4] Rosenberg 2015, p. 25
[5] Ibid., pp. 28, 32

An evaluation generalizes and casts judgment:

- Mary, what you said was rude.
- Paul, you are not good at sales.

Evaluations and judgments obscure what happened. If I say, "Mary, what you said was rude," I am not sharing what occurred. I am sharing my judgment of what occurred. NVC encourages us to share what we observed and *then* share our feelings about it.

Identifying and communicating our feelings

My teammate, Casey Cumbow, first introduced Lessonly to NVC. While leading a workshop on the four components, she summarized why it's so important to recognize and communicate our feelings:

Feelings tell us if our needs are being met. By training ourselves to be more mindful of our feelings and more aware of the nuances of feelings, we gain a greater understanding of—and connection with—ourselves. Empathy is the ability to understand and share the feelings of another. So, if we can't identify our feelings and share them, we make it impossible for others to empathize with us. If you say you are agitated, I know what it is like to feel agitated, so I can now appreciate how you feel.

Indeed, if we want to be understood, we must first help people understand us. Let's continue the Mary and Paul examples and add *feelings* to each observation:

- Mary, during the team meeting, you said I was slowing you down. I did not know that, and *I felt upset and embarrassed when I heard it.*
- Paul, you have not closed a deal in seven months. *I am worried about this.*

When we observe—"Paul, you have not closed a deal in seven months."—and share how we personally feel about our observation—"I am worried about this."—we get somewhere! Paul can hear us, because we've taken the time to be clear about the actual thing that's going on and the relatable emotion we are feeling in response to it.

Here are two things to keep in mind as we learn to communicate our feelings:

1. We are responsible for how we feel.

When we say, "That makes me feel . . . " we are not taking responsibility for our feelings. Instead, we are acting as if someone or something else is in control of how we feel. An important part of NVC is working to break this habit by recognizing you and I are responsible for how we feel. We can reflect this in our speech by replacing, "Matt doesn't care about me. He is *making me* angry," with, *"I am* angry Matt did not ask if I needed help."

2. Feelings are different from thoughts.

We often preface our thoughts with "I feel . . . " But thoughts are different from feelings. When we say, "I feel like you aren't pulling your weight on the team," we are expressing a thought (a personal perspective), not a feeling (a universal emotion). To take this thought and translate it into a feeling, we would say: "I haven't heard from you for six days. *I am hurt and overwhelmed.*"

Rosenberg has a good rule of thumb for knowing whether we are expressing a feeling or a thought: Try to replace "I feel" with "I am." For example, "I feel sad" can just as easily be "I am sad." If you can't replace *I feel* with *I am*, you may be expressing a thought—most often, a judgment—instead of a feeling.

When I first learned about NVC, I found it helpful to review Rosenberg's list of feelings,[6] so I've re-published part of it below. It's not exhaustive, but it will be useful as you seek to identify and share your feelings.

How we are likely to feel
when our needs are being met:

Affectionate, amazed, amused, appreciative, astonished, buoyant, calm, carefree, comfortable, complacent, confident, contented, curious, dazzled, delighted, eager, ecstatic, encouraged, energetic, enthusiastic, excited, exhilarated, expectant, fascinated, free, friendly, fulfilled, gleeful, good-humored, grateful, happy, helpful, hopeful, inquisitive, inspired, intense, interested, intrigued, invigorated, joyful, jubilant, loving, mellow, merry, moved, optimistic, overwhelmed, peaceful, pleasant, pleased, proud, quiet, radiant, refreshed, relaxed, relieved, satisfied, secure, sensitive, stimulated, surprised, tender, thankful, thrilled, touched, tranquil, trusting, upbeat, warm, wide-awake, zestful

---

[6] Rosenberg 2015, pp. 44–45

How we are likely to feel when our needs are not being met:

Afraid, agitated, alarmed, aloof, angry, annoyed, anxious, apathetic, ashamed, bewildered, bitter, blah, blue, bored, brokenhearted, cold, concerned, dejected, depressed, despairing, detached, disappointed, disenchanted, disgruntled, disgusted, disheartened, displeased, distressed, disturbed, downcast, dull, edgy, embarrassed, exasperated, exhausted, fidgety, forlorn, frightened, frustrated, furious, gloomy, guilty, heavy, helpless, hesitant, horrified, hostile, humdrum, hurt, impatient, indifferent, intense, irate, irked, irritated, jealous, lazy, lethargic, listless, lonely, mad, mean, miserable, mopey, mournful, nervous, numb, overwhelmed, panicky, perplexed, pessimistic, puzzled, reluctant, repelled, resentful, sad, scared, sensitive, shaky, skeptical, sorrowful, sorry, startled, suspicious, terrified, tired, troubled, uncomfortable, unconcerned, uneasy, unglued, unhappy, unsteady, upset, uptight, weary, wistful, withdrawn, worried

Identifying and communicating our needs

Our feelings are rooted in our needs. When our needs are being met, we feel positive emotions (comfortable, optimistic, thankful). When our needs are *not* being met, we feel negative emotions (nervous, scared, agitated). NVC describes needs as universal human qualities without reference to place, person, or time, and reminds us that our needs are no more or less important than the needs of anyone else.

When we connect our feelings to our needs, we continue to help people understand and support us. Rosenberg acknowledges how difficult this is:

> Unfortunately, most of us have never been taught to think in terms of needs. We are accustomed to thinking about what's wrong with other people when our needs aren't being fulfilled. Thus, if we want coats to be hung up in the closet, we may characterize our children as lazy for leaving them on the couch. Or we may interpret our co-workers as irresponsible when they don't go about their tasks the way we would prefer them to.[7]

---

[7] Rosenberg 2015, p. 53

Let's continue the Mary and Paul examples. As a reminder, here were our initial evaluations:

- Mary, what you said was rude.
- Paul, you are not good at sales.

And here's the NVC way, with our observations, feelings, and *needs*:

- Mary, during the team meeting, you said I was slowing you down. I did not know that, and I felt upset and embarrassed when I heard it. *I value communication and trust.*

- Paul, you have not closed a deal in seven months. I am worried about this, because *I value consistency and support.*

Look at how much clearer the NVC way is when compared with our original evaluations. This is how we connect and make progress together!

In *Nonviolent Communication*, Rosenberg recalls his mother attending one of his workshops and becoming upset:

I asked, "Mother, are you all right?"

"Yes," she answered, "but I just had a sudden realization that's very hard for me to take in."

"What's that?"

"I've just become aware that for thirty-six years, I was angry with your father for not meeting my needs, and now I realize that I never once clearly told him what I needed."

My mother's revelation was accurate. Not one time, that I can remember, did she clearly express her needs to my father. She'd hint around and go through all kinds of convolutions, but never would she ask directly for what she needed. . . . It has been my experience over and over again that from the moment people begin talking about what they need rather than what's wrong with one another, the possibility of finding ways to meet everybody's needs is greatly increased.[8]

Is this something you can relate to? We go through life expecting a lot of others, but we don't always fill them in. NVC is another way to bring clarity to our relationships.

[8] Rosenberg 2015, pp. 54, 56

Rosenberg and his team also put together a list of needs.[9] I've republished it below. Like the list of feelings, it is not exhaustive, but it can be useful as you seek to map your feelings to your needs.

Connection: acceptance, affection, appreciation, belonging, cooperation, communication, closeness, community, companionship, compassion, consideration, consistency, empathy, inclusion, intimacy, love, mutuality, nurturing, respect/self-respect, safety, security, stability, support, to know and be known, to see and be seen, to understand and be understood, trust, warmth

Physical Well-Being: air, food, movement/exercise, rest/sleep, sexual expression, safety, shelter, touch, water

Honesty: authenticity, integrity, presence

---

[9]   Rosenberg 2015, pp. 54–55

Play: joy, humor

Peace: beauty, communion, ease, equality, harmony, inspiration, order

Autonomy: choice, freedom, independence, space, spontaneity

Meaning: awareness, celebration of life, challenge, clarity, competence, consciousness, contribution, creativity, discovery, efficacy, effectiveness, growth, hope, learning, mourning, participation, purpose, self-expression, stimulation, to matter, understanding

Making specific and empathetic requests

The fourth component of NVC is requests. *Requests* help others see how they can meet our needs. They usually involve a particular person doing a particular thing at a particular time:

- Mary, during the team meeting, you said I was slowing you down. I did not know that, and I felt upset and embarrassed when I heard it. I value communication and trust, so *going forward, if you are wanting something from me, can we talk about it one-on-one first?*

- Paul, you have not closed a deal in seven months. I am worried about this, because I value consistency and support. *My request is that you meet these specific performance goals next month* if you would like to continue being on the sales team.

Requests should not be demands. We should never guilt, shame, manipulate, or threaten people into doing what we want. Everyone should know they have the choice to *not* do what we are asking. Otherwise, their actions are not motivated by their hearts, but by their guilt, shame, or fear.

In the examples above, we are not saying Mary will be punished if she doesn't meet our request. We are simply asking for her help. And while it is true that Paul cannot keep missing his sales numbers and remain on the team, it is also true that he can choose not to work toward the performance goals if he'd rather not. In both cases, we can offer additional communication to clarify that we *empathize with the needs of others* as we seek to have our own needs met:

- Mary, during the team meeting, you said I was slowing you down. I did not know that, and I felt upset and embarrassed when I heard it. I value communication and trust, so going forward, if you are needing something from me, can we talk about it one-on-one first? *And later this week, would you like to discuss where I might be able to provide more support?*

- Paul, you have not closed a deal in seven months. I am worried about this, because I value consistency and support. My request is that you meet these specific performance goals next month if you would like to continue being on the sales team. *I do understand that you also value stability and consistency in your life, so if you would prefer, we can start working together right now to help you find another role here or elsewhere.*

When you make requests, be specific, and for best results, show empathy for the other person's needs too.

After a difficult conversation, make sure you both heard one another

It's common to finish a difficult conversation and worry you misunderstood the other person's message or weren't as clear as you intended to be. All the adrenaline of the moment can make it hard to remember what was said clearly, or even said at all. That's why, when you're wrapping up a difficult conversation, reflect back what you heard the other person say, and ask if they would be open to returning the favor. It's important to not assume your messages were perfectly communicated or understood, especially in moments when tensions were high. If it makes more sense to recap the conversation the next day, once everyone's had time to process it, that works great too.[10]

Wrapping up

We turn conflict into an advantage when we communicate through it and learn from it. Having compassionate conversations when circumstances become difficult is an important

---

[10] This concludes our primer on the NVC process. Once again, I would like to thank Dr. Rosenberg's estate for letting me share his wisdom. It is a great privilege. I encourage everyone to read the third edition of *Nonviolent Communication: A Language of Life*. There's a lot more to NVC than we covered here. And frankly, nothing compares to learning it from the man himself.

part of being a good teammate, doing better work, and living a better life. We need to talk through our observations, feelings, needs, and requests so we can find resolutions that are supportive of ourselves and others. None of this is easy, but it's worth every second of practice.

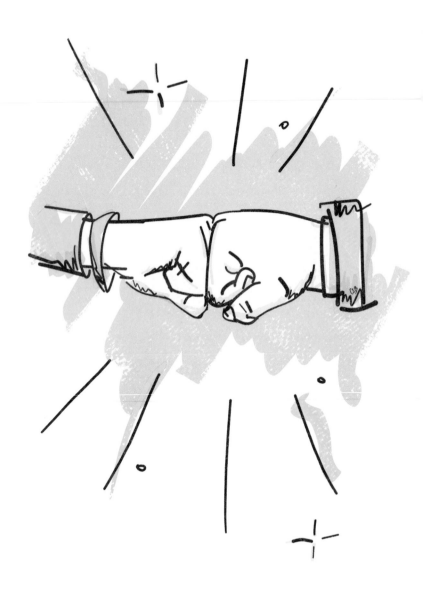

Chapter 7

Get More Agreements

Make time to agree on
the behaviors you want to see.

I want my relationships to be full of mutual trust and respect. My teammates do too. So when we heard Steve Chandler's wisdom on expectations versus agreements,[1] we started on an important mission: fewer expectations and more agreements. And you know what? Work is much better now.

Why we want fewer expectations

*An **expectation** is a belief somebody will or should do something.*

---

[1] Chandler 2012

There's a lot to dislike about expectations. For one, they rarely have upside. When you expect something from me, there are two predominant outcomes, and both are underwhelming:

Outcome 1: I'll meet your expectations, and you'll think, *I expected that.*

Outcome 2: I'll fall short of your expectations, and you'll think, *I am disappointed.*

Expectations make it hard for us to win and celebrate together, and they allow me to skip the parts where:

1. I have to be clear with you about what I want.
2. You get to acknowledge you understand and are open to participating in what I want.
3. You negotiate your wants with me so we can find common ground and mutual benefit.

With expectations, I get to sit back and hold you accountable for something you might not even know about.

Here are some examples of expectations:

- Jamie expects his vendors to check in with him twice a month. The vendors don't know that, but he sure does.

- Grant thinks his boss should consider him for a raise. He's waiting for his boss to come to the same conclusion.
- Noelle manages Bob and expects him to call her if he is going to be late. Noelle thinks this is a basic procedure Bob should be aware of.

Scenarios like these are ripe for distress and resentment. Luckily for us, there's a better way.

Why we want more agreements

*An **agreement** is a negotiated arrangement between people that defines a course of action and each person's responsibility within it.*

Agreements have upside for the both of us. When you and I agree on something, we replace soul-sucking assumptions with life-giving cooperation. Agreements help us clarify our relationship so we both understand what we're after and how we'll get there. They take what could otherwise be left to presumption and help us make it explicit through communication. When we make agreements, we demonstrate respect and care for one another and set ourselves up for success everyone can celebrate.

Here are some examples of agreements:

- Jamie expects his vendors to check in with him twice a month, so he asks each vendor if they can accommodate his request. They all agree.
- Grant asks his boss if she'd be open to discussing his compensation. She says, "Of course." They schedule the meeting.
- Noelle asks Bob, "Hey, can you agree to call me if you're running late, and I'll do the same for you if I'm running late?" Bob says, "You got it!"

Agreements allow us to hold one another accountable in a way that is fair. If Bob shows up late again without calling, Noelle has common ground to stand on when she feels agitated. She can pull Bob aside and say, "You agreed to call me when you were running late. I am frustrated you didn't do that today. I value communication. What happened?"

Whether you're a manager or not, having common ground to stand on is a valuable aspect of agreements. If you see a teammate doing something and you want it to change, instead of being upset, ask your teammate if they'd be open to a different approach. Suggest your desired approach and, if possible, explain why you think it's mutually beneficial. Then, give your teammate a chance to offer their own suggestions.

Work together to find common ground and, once you do, agree on it. If one of you ever forgets about the agreement, you can always reorient by saying, "If possible, I would really like to stick to our agreement here."[2]

Here are some examples of this approach:

- Leo, next time a customer makes a similar request, I would prefer we clear it with the finance team first, since we ultimately need their approval. Going forward, are you good with that approach?

- Tori, going forward, could you acknowledge receipt of the invoice emails I send your way? I worry when I don't know if you've seen them.

- Jay, going forward, if a team needs something edited, can we agree to a 48-hour turnaround time? That amount of time ensures we do a thorough job with our proofreading.

- Mary, during the team meeting, you said I was slowing you down. I did not know that, and I felt upset and

---

[2] There will be times when agreements need to be modified. We'll cover that soon.

embarrassed when I heard it. I value communication and trust, so going forward, if you are wanting something from me, can we talk about it one-on-one first? (This example is from chapter 6.)

More examples of what it looks like to get agreements

Here's an example where Lena and her teammate, Tom, put in the effort to make a multi-layered agreement. During their conversation, you'll notice there are many occasions for them to assume they are aligned, but they always go the extra mile to clarify responsibilities and timelines:

Tom: Hey, Lena, I need a design done by 5pm on Monday, July 21, so I can have it ready for a meeting the next morning (Tuesday, July 22). Do you have the capacity to help with this?

Lena: Sure, Tom, I'd be happy to help if I can. Do you have an example of what the design will look like? I'll need that before I can commit to a timeline.

Tom: (sharing an example) It will need to look something like this.

Lena: Got it, thanks! And will I be writing the text, or will you provide it?

Tom: I'll provide it.

Lena: Perfect. When will you be sending it to me?

Tom: You mean the text? I'll write and send it before noon tomorrow.

Lena: Great. To get this done by Monday, July 21, I will need to drop everything I'm currently working on. So I won't be able to get Project A or Project B done on time. Is that okay with you?

Tom: I wish I could push back those projects, but we can't. What do you recommend?

Lena: Can you push the meeting back three days to Friday, July 25? If so, I can keep everything on schedule and get this new project done by 5pm on July 24.

Tom: Okay, I just asked. We can push the meeting to Friday.

Lena: Great, do you want to review anything before I send the design your way on Thursday?

Tom: Yeah, can you send me a draft earlier in the day— sometime before noon?

Lena: Yes, I'll need your comments by 1pm that day so I have enough time to address them.

Tom: You got it.

Lena: Awesome, so here's my attempt at a summary: You'll get me the text by noon tomorrow. I'll finish a first draft of the design before noon on July 24 and send it to you. You'll get me any comments before 1pm on July 24, and then I'll send you a final draft later that same day, before 5pm. Can you confirm that all this is accurate?

Tom: Yes, that's all correct. Thanks a lot, Lena.

Lena: Perfect, you are welcome!

By explicitly agreeing to the details of Tom's request (deliverables, timeline, review process, etc.) and recapping the agreement at the end of the conversation, Lena and Tom have minimized assumptions and maximized alignment. This is the kind of work that pays itself back in spades. A few extra minutes to demonstrate camaraderie and foster more clarity is a few extra minutes well spent.

Take responsibility for writing down a verbal agreement

If you made your agreement verbally and need it to stand the test of time, take responsibility for recapping it in writing. Things are easily lost in translation or forgotten with each passing day. A written recap that everyone can validate and revisit is immensely helpful.

Take responsibility whenever and however an agreement breaks down

People with the best intentions fall short of their agreements. You will do it, and so will others. Here's how to handle these situations, no matter who drops the ball.

When you fall short of an agreement, don't make an excuse. Just say, "I am sorry I dropped the ball here." Then, decide if you should renew or modify the agreement. If you want to renew the agreement but aren't sure how, ask the person, "What can I do to get our agreement back on track? Here's an idea I had: [insert idea for getting the agreement back on track]. What do you think?" If you want to modify the agreement, say what aspects you'd like to adjust, explain why, and ask the other person how they feel about the changes. If you've learned you don't have the capacity to do what you thought you could do, that's life—own it. Say, "I realize now I should not have committed to this. I no longer believe I can reliably get it done. How can I make it up to you?" The other person might be hurt to hear you say this, but I hope they will both forgive you and appreciate your honesty. Many people ignore or dance around their overcommitments. It is always more courageous to own up to them.

When the other person falls short of an agreement, own the process for getting things back on track. Like Grant in the earlier example, a friend of mine once asked her boss about a raise. Her boss said they could talk about it in November. November came and went and nothing happened. My friend assumed her boss's lack of follow-up was purposeful, so she didn't broach the topic again. My advice: Don't go this route. When you get an agreement with someone, don't be shy about following up on it. You can be graceful and hold people accountable at the same time. Here's how:

Step 1. Take responsibility, even if the other person doesn't. Rather than waiting for the other person to realize they've dropped a ball—or worse, letting blame and frustration build up within you—talk to the person who isn't meeting their end of the agreement. Be kind and assume they meant no harm. When my friend's raise conversation came and went, instead of remaining quiet, she could have said, "Hey, just checking in. We agreed to talk about a raise in November. Can we agree to talk about it this month instead? If so, what day and time works best for you? Thanks so much!"

Step 2. Offer to help. And when you do, ditch the hollow phrase, "Let me know if I can help," and replace it with specific ways you can pitch in. Say something like, "I am sure there's a lot going on right now. Just want you to know, if it helps, I would be happy to [insert one or more things you could do to potentially alleviate the person's stress]." This subtle but important upgrade proves you're not just going through the motions. You're willing to take an extra minute to consider the person's situation and identify places you can offer support. It's little, but it's big.

Here's an example of Lena owning the agreement after Tom missed the agreed-upon window for providing edits:

Lena: Hey, Tom, hope you are well! I sent you a draft of the design this morning, but I haven't seen your comments come back yet and it's almost 1pm. We agreed to get comments in by 1pm so I can finish by 5pm today. Do you have any updates?

Tom: Sorry Lena, today has been crazy and I totally forgot! I haven't had a chance to look yet.

Lena: I totally get it, but I am nervous about meeting my 5pm deadline. Would it be helpful for me to get feedback from someone else on the team—maybe Adam or Helen?

Tom: Thanks for offering and sorry again. I'm just getting out of a meeting, but I can comment and send to you by 1:45pm. Is that still enough time to meet the deadline?

Lena: Yes, I can make that work!

Tom: I so appreciate it. Thanks for reminding me and being flexible!

People forget. Sometimes they are overworked. Sometimes they are not intentional enough about their commitments. Take a generous posture and do your part to follow up. Twiddling your thumbs or complaining about your absent-minded teammates won't bring camaraderie or progress to anything. Be the person you'd want to work with. Assume good things about people, forgive them when they mess up, identify ways you might help, and don't pass the buck—even when you have a reason to do so.[3]

Wrapping up

Make a point to *expect* less and *agree* more. This subtle but important shift in posture will bring you closer to your teammates and your goals, while helping you hold yourself and others accountable in a way that is considerate and clear.

---

[3] In his autobiography, Benjamin Franklin caught himself rationalizing his own behavior and wrote, "So convenient a thing it is to be a reasonable creature, since it enables one to find or make a reason for every thing one has a mind to do." (Franklin 1791, p. 51) We can always come up with a reason not to do the work or not to lend the hand. Reasons are abundant and easy. Commit to following up and following through anyway.

Chapter 8

Bring Brightness to the Room

Showing up is important,
but how you show up matters more.

Statler and Waldorf are Muppets. They are known for their first-rate theater seats, where they mock or celebrate whatever show they've just seen. I have a recording from one of their sketches I like to listen to. It demonstrates how contagious emotions can be. Statler begins by booing the performance, so Waldorf does the same. They call the show "horrendous" and "terrible." Then Waldorf changes his tune: "Well it wasn't that bad." Statler agrees: "Yeah, it was *good* actually." This continues until both Muppets are cheering the performance, shouting, "Bravo!" and "More, more!"

Have you ever experienced a moment where one person's enthusiasm or dissatisfaction guides the rest of the room? Maybe you just announced a big change, kicked off a group project, or sat down for a routine meeting. It's times like these when all it takes to shape a group's perspective is someone freely sharing how they feel about the matter at hand. A remark of, "This is exciting!" elevates the room, bringing momentum to the moment. A remark of, "Do we have to?" causes everyone to downshift and dig their heels in. Nonverbals do the same. An unimpressed look or the checking of a cell phone can signal a moment is boring or inconsequential.

Celebrating and rewarding people who bring excitement and positivity to their work is a good way to get others to do the same. But the main thing you control in moments like these is what *you* bring to a room. So how do you show up? Do you bring cheer? Warmth? Indifference? Friction? If you're like me, on your good days you bring the first two, and on your bad days you bring the last two.

In *The Culture Code*, Daniel Coyle cites research by Will Felps[1] that has me working harder to summon cheer and

[1] Felps is an associate professor at the University of New South Wales in Australia.

warmth in the moment—even when I'm not feeling like my best self.

In Felps's experiments, participants are brought together under the pretense of creating a marketing plan for a startup. A young man named Nick is planted in each group. He's there to be subtly disruptive so Felps can measure just how sensitive the group is to a single person's attitude. In each run of the experiment, Nick plays one of three roles—the Jerk, the Slacker, or the Downer. Without fail, his presence negatively impacts the group's performance by 30 to 40 percent. At no time is Nick called out as the leader of the group. As far as anyone knows, he's just another randomly selected participant, but his attitude matters all the same.

Going into the project, Felps imagined people would get upset with Nick's behavior, but they didn't. Instead, Felps said, the participants' vibe was, "If that's how it is, then we'll be Slackers and Downers too."[2]

Does this mean all hope is lost if we get one Nick in a group? The good news is, maybe not! One particular group was able to rise above Nick's negative behaviors and successfully complete

---

[2] Coyle 2018, p. 2

the project. Felps attributed the group's success to the "almost invisible"[3] techniques of a participant named Jonathan:

> Nick behaves like a jerk, and Jonathan reacts instantly with warmth, deflecting the negativity and making a potentially unstable situation feel solid and safe. Then Jonathan pivots and asks a simple question that draws others out, and he listens intently and responds. Energy levels increase; people open up and share ideas, building chains of insight and cooperation that move the group swiftly and steadily toward the goal.[4]

Felps summarized Jonathan's impact:

> Basically, [Jonathan] makes it safe, then turns to the other people and asks, "Hey, what do you think of this?" . . . Sometimes he even asks Nick questions like, "How would you do that?" Most of all he radiates an idea that is something like, *Hey, this is all really comfortable and engaging and I'm curious what everybody else has to say.* It was amazing how such small behaviors kept everybody engaged and on task.[5]

---

[3] Coyle 2018, p. 5
[4] Ibid.
[5] Ibid., pp. 5–6

If you ever come over to the Yoder household for dinner, you're likely to hear this story. It's too important not to share, because it has implications for us all. No matter your rank or role, you have the power to bring better work out of people.

You might be wondering how far these results stretch. Is the contagiousness of our emotions a matter of proximity? Do we have to be physically in a room together to affect the moods and perspectives of others? In a world where work gets done via text message and group chat, does the way we digitally show up also matter? The short answer is yes.

Back in 2014, Facebook was widely criticized for running an experiment on an unwitting subset of its users. As reported by *The New York Times*, Facebook's Core Data Science Team "manipulated the news feeds of over half a million randomly selected users to change the number of positive and negative posts they saw. It was part of a psychological study to examine how emotions can be spread on social media."[6]

The Facebook team summarized its findings in an article:

Emotional states can be transferred to others via emotional contagion, leading people to experience the same emotions

---

[6] Goel 2014

without their awareness. Emotional contagion is well established in laboratory experiments, with people transferring positive and negative emotions to others. . . . In an experiment with people who use Facebook, we test whether emotional contagion occurs outside of in-person interaction between individuals by reducing the amount of emotional content in the News Feed. When positive expressions were reduced, people produced fewer positive posts and more negative posts; when negative expressions were reduced, the opposite pattern occurred. These results indicate that emotions expressed by others on Facebook influence our own emotions.[7]

If this information motivates you to distance yourself from the perennial downers who frequent your online and offline social networks, I don't blame you. Their complaints and gloomy forecasts aren't just passive annoyances—they affect how you feel. You know better than to hang out with a person who repeatedly punches you in your gut. How about a person who repeatedly punches you in your mood?

---

[7] Kramer, Guillory, & Hancock 2014

On the brighter side of this research, we have yet another reason to share our love, appreciation (chapter 5), and optimism with the world. Positive sentiments spread just the same.

Wrapping up

One of the most important things you can do is become more aware of how you show up. Do you bring cheer? Warmth? Indifference? Friction? Something else? Are you more often a Nick or a Jonathan? Do you kneecap progress or accelerate it? And now that you know how much it matters, will you make a point to bring more excitement, warmth, and encouragement to the people you interact with? Your attitude and openness could be the difference between someone smiling or frowning, or a group achieving progress or paralysis. It turns out we all have great power over others. How will you use yours?

Epilogue

Better work and better lives
have a lot in common.

Nassim Taleb taught me the concept of antifragility (chapter 6). He also taught me about domain dependence,[1] which explains how people struggle in taking a lesson from one context and applying it to another. My own domain dependence popped up when I was writing songs for a recent album (I make music for fun). I worked on my songs in a vacuum—just like I had with Quipol—and experienced similarly discouraging results. I polished things I should have cut, cut things I should have kept, and wound up with songs that didn't work. My context

[1] Taleb 2012, pp. 38–40

had changed, and I'd forgotten the lesson of share before you're ready (chapter 2).

It's with domain dependence in mind that I write my farewell. I hinted at it throughout this book, but now that we are wrapping up, I want to make sure it's clear. All these lessons about doing better work also apply to living a better life. They work just as well in a living room as they do in a conference room.

With that said . . .

I hope the next time you face hardship or are in need, you will be vulnerable, look for opportunity, and have difficult conversations.

I hope the next time you want to do something meaningful for someone else, you will share before you're ready.

I hope the next time you feel confused or want to know more, you will ask clarifying questions.

I hope the next time you see your friends and family, you will highlight what's working in your relationships.

I hope the next time someone depends on you—or you depend on someone else—you will get more agreements.

And I hope you will bring brightness to as many rooms as you can.

Our influence boils down to what we do and what we celebrate. So let me leave you with one last question: What do you do and what do you celebrate? My greatest hope is you'll do better work, live a better life, and celebrate when others do the same.

Acknowledgments

People who reviewed or otherwise gave life to these ideas

My parents, Luann and Robin Yoder, as well as Adam Neddo, Alex Bantz, Alex Castaneda, Alex Lau, Alex Mislan, Alex O'Cull, Alex Wilhelm, Alex Yoder, Alli Webb, Aman Brar, Anderson Garland, Andrew Robinson III, Andy Hall, Ann Johnston, Anthony Garber, Barry Wormser, Ben Battaglia, Blake Koriath, Bob Carlson, Brad Feld, Brad Wisler, Brian Millis, Brock Benefiel, Brody Bernheisel, Bruce Pavitt, Bryan Naas, Carol Farrell, Carol Weiss-Kennedy, Carol Kennedy-Armbruster, Caryssa Perez, Casey Cumbow, Charles Oexmann, Chelsey Pietropaolo, Chris Baggott, Chris Byers, Claudia Reuter, Coco Brown, Cody Coppotelli, Colin Yoder, Collin Stanley, Conlin Durbin, Conner Burt, Cooper Garland, Corey Kime, Dan Kennedy, Daniel Thang, Danielle Coppotelli, Dave Kendall, Don Aquilano, Don Sobaski, Doug Stanley, Drake Oversen, Drew Marquardt, Dustin Sapp, Elizabeth Yoder, Eric Beers, Erica Raeber, Erin Silverling, Evan Wible, Fred Wilson, Helen

Gardner, Holden Yoder, Jacey Liechty, Jackie Wormser, Jason Marcuson, Jay Baer, Jeb Banner, Jennifer Manning, Jeremy Huckins, Jess Yoder, Jill Bolte Taylor, Jim Pike, Joe Farrell, Joe Farquharson, Joe Konopa, Joel Book, Joel Pietropaolo, John Hunckler, John Talbott, John Yoder, Jon Hubartt, Jon Showalter, Jordan Burt, Judy Dalka, Justin Kime, Justin Moses, Karlie Briggs, Katie Brunette, Katie Townsend, Kay Stanley, Kristian Andersen, Kristin Garland, Kyle Jackson, Kyle Lacy, Kyle Roach, Laura John, Lauren Stebbins, Lena Burt, Leo Castaneda, Luca Castaneda, Luke Jacobs, Maggie Castaneda, Mallary Kineman, Margie Fultz, Marisa Yoder, Marty Armbruster, Matt Caudill, Matt Hunckler, Matt Lubbers, Maxwell Perkins, Megan Jarvis, Megan Mioduski, Michael Walden, Michelle Bower, Mike Fitzgerald, Mike Overpeck, Mike Preuss, Mike Trotzke, Mike Wendahl, Mikey Mioduski, Mitch Causey, Morgan Polizzi, Nataly Kogan, Nathan Sinsabaugh, Nick Croyle, Nickolas Kramer, Nicole Schneider, Pete Gall, Rachel Saltsgaver, Rick Grey, Ricky Pelletier, Rita Troyer, Ross Lubbers, Ross Reinhardt, Sarah Battaglia, Scott Cook, Scott Dorsey, Scott Fitzgerald, Scott Maxwell, Sean Costello, Shannon Garland, Spencer Oversen, Stacy Hiquet, Stella Garland, Stephanie Martin, Steve Krahnke, Steven Emch, Tamara Green, Tanner Steel, Tara Overpeck, Tim Blaum, Tyler Coppotelli, Ursula LaFosse, Waseem Dahman, and Zach McFarlen.

Bibliography

Chandler, Steve. *Choices for a More Powerful You*. 2012, http://www.stevechandler.com/choices.html.

Coyle, Daniel. *The Culture Code: The Hidden Language of Highly Successful Groups*. New York, NY: Bantam, 2017.

DC Comics. "DC Reveals Tom King and Clay Mann's Top Secret Project, Sanctuary, as 'Heroes in Crisis'." News release, June 13, 2018. DC Comics. Accessed December 8, 2018. https://www.dccomics.com/blog/2018/06/13/dc-reveals-tom-king-and-clay-manns-top-secret-project-sanctuary-as-heroes-in.

Drucker, Peter F. *The Effective Executive*. New York, NY: Harper & Row, 1967.

Franklin, Benjamin. *Autobiography of Benjamin Franklin*. New York, NY: MacMillan, 1791.

Froyd, Jeff, and Jean Layne. "Faculty Development Strategies for Overcoming the 'Curse of Knowledge'." In *2008 38th Annual Frontiers in Education Conference* (October 2008): S4D-13-S4D-16. https://doi.org/10.1109/fie.2008.4720529.

Goel, Vindu. "Facebook Tinkers With Users' Emotions in News Feed Experiment, Stirring Outcry." *The New York Times*, June 30, 2014. June 29, 2014. Accessed December 8, 2018. https://www.nytimes.com/2014/06/30/technology/facebook-tinkers-with-users-emotions-in-news-feed-experiment-stirring-outcry.html.

Haidt, Jonathan. *The Happiness Hypothesis: Finding Modern Truth in Ancient Wisdom*. New York, NY: Basic Books, 2006.

Hammond, Sue Annis. *The Thin Book of Appreciative Inquiry*. 3rd ed. Bend, OR: Thin Book Publishing, 2013.

Hendrek, Oalar. "What Will 'Jaws' And 'Exorcist' Do For an Encore?" *The New York Times*, June 27, 1976. June 27, 1976. Accessed December 8, 2018. https://www.nytimes.com/1976/06/27/archives/what-will-jaws-and-exorcist-do-for-an-encore.html.

Ito, Tiffany A., Jeff T. Larsen, Kyle Smith, and John T. Cacioppo. "Negative Information Weighs More Heavily on the Brain: The Negativity Bias in Evaluative Categorizations." *Journal of Personality and Social Psychology* 75, no. 4 (1998): 887–900.

Jaws: The Inside Story. Produced by Kevin Bachar, Robert Sharenow, Peter Tarshis, Tom Moody, Amelia Hanibelsz, and Georgia Manukas. By Rob Goldberg. United States: Pangolin, 2010.

Kay, Roz. "Positive Change: The Art of Appreciative Inquiry with David Cooperrider." *Inside Transformational Leadership*. Podcast audio, January 25, 2016. https://itunes.apple.com/us/podcast/inside-transformational-leadership/id955709779.

Kramer, Adam D.I., Jamie E. Guillory, and Jeffery T. Hancock. "Experimental Evidence of Massive-Scale Emotional Contagion through Social Networks." *Proceedings of the National Academy of Sciences* 111, no. 24 (June 2, 2014): 8788–8790. June 17, 2014. Accessed December 8, 2018. https://doi.org/10.1073/pnas.1320040111.

Lakoff, George, and Mark Johnson. *Metaphors We Live By*. Chicago, IL: University of Chicago Press, 2003.

Pals, Jennifer L., and Dan P. McAdams. "The Transformed Self: A Narrative Understanding of Posttraumatic Growth." *Psychological Inquiry* 15, no. 1 (2004): 65–69. https://www.jstor.org/stable/20447204.

Pennebaker, James W., and Joshua M. Smyth. *Opening Up by Writing It Down: How Expressive Writing Improves Health and Eases Emotional Pain.* New York, NY: Guilford Press, 2016.

Pinker, Steven. *Enlightenment Now.* New York, NY: Viking Penguin, 2018.

Pinker, Steven. *The Sense of Style: The Thinking Person's Guide to Writing in the 21st Century.* New York, NY: Viking Penguin, 2014.

Rosenberg, Marshall B. *Nonviolent Communication: A Language of Life.* 3rd ed. Encinitas, CA: PuddleDancer Press, 2015.

She Wore a Yellow Ribbon. Directed by John Ford. By Frank S. Nugent. Performed by John Wayne, Joanne Dru, John Agar, and Ben Johnson. United States: RKO Radio Pictures, Inc., 1949.

Spielberg. Produced by Susan Lacy, Jessica Levin, and Emma Pildes. United States: HBO Documentary Films and Pentimento Productions, 2017.

Taleb, Nassim. *Antifragile: Things that Gain from Disorder*. New York, NY: Random House, 2012.

Taylor, Jill Bolte. "Building a Better Brain." Lecture, Yellowship, The Mavris Arts & Event Center, Indianapolis, IN, April 19, 2018.

Turner, Cory. "Hunting Bruce, Or, On The Trail Of The 'Jaws' Shark." *NPR* (audio blog), June 2, 2010. Accessed December 2, 2018. https://www.npr.org/templates/transcript/transcript.php?storyId=127370664.

About the Type

The body of this book is set in Adobe Garamond Pro. The Adobe Garamond™ font family is based on the typefaces of famed sixteenth-century Parisian printer Claude Garamond. Its italics are influenced by the designs of Garamond's assistant, Robert Granjon. Because Adobe Garamond's letterforms use less ink than similar faces, it's not just a beautiful, highly readable typeface, but an eco-friendly one, too.

The chapter titles, subtitles, and headers are set in Montserrat, which was created by Argentinian type designer Julieta Ulanovsky and named after the first and oldest neighborhood in Buenos Aires, where Ulanovsky still lives and works. The typeface was inspired by the typographic signage that lined the streets of Montserrat in the early twentieth century.

The handwriting is by Helen Gardner, designer and illustrator of this book.